Welcome

Hi friends!

I'm so glad you've decided to invest in your marriage. I think we can all agree that some days, marriage seems impossible... but with God, we know that ALL things are possible!

Marriage requires a whole lot of work and intention, and we could all use a few handy tools to help us figure out what to do and where to grow. That's where The Marriage Builder Toolkit comes in!

In the following pages, you'll find a ton of resources to help you as you focus on building up your marriage & intentionally loving your spouse. I'm so thrilled that you're taking the time to work on your marriage, and I pray that you'll find these pages helpful and encouraging!

I'm praying for you and your spouse, that God would work in your marriage to make each of you more like God's Spirit.

Blessings,

Diana Asaad & The MMI Team

As always, please email us if you have any questions or suggestions. You can reach us at Info@MyMarriageIntensive.com

Table of Contents

Monthly Prayer Calendar

Praying is an important weapon we can use to fight the enemy and to strengthen our relationship.

We highly encourage couples to spend some time in daily prayer.

Listed below are ideas that will help you, remind you, and encourage you to pray for each other.

We recommend that couples take turns praying for each other.

Feel free to use the suggested topics or you can choose your own topic based on how you feel or how your day is going.

Day 1	Day 2	Day 3	Day 4	Day 5	Day 6	Day 7
Integrity	Relationship with the Lord	Unity	Love for each other	Compassion	Parenthood/ Family	Encouraging Words
Day 8	**Day 9**	**Day 10**	**Day 11**	**Day 12**	**Day 13**	**Day 14**
Forgiveness	Purposeful Work	Peace	Wisdom	Selflessness	Faithfulness	Extended Family
Day 15	**Day 16**	**Day 17**	**Day 18**	**Day 19**	**Day 20**	**Day 21**
Joy	Connection	Time in the Word	Gentleness	Patience	Faithfulness	Goodness
Day 22	**Day 23**	**Day 24**	**Day 25**	**Day 26**	**Day 27**	**Day 28**
Self-Control	Strength	Purpose	A Tame Tongue	Health	Humility	Needs met
Day 29	*Day 30*	*Day 31*				
Identity	*Strength*	*Favor*				

Date Night Planner

Sometimes, date night comes around and both spouses look at each other wondering what to do when where to go. This list takes care of all those questions ahead of time! Keep this list handy, add to it when you think of something fun to do, and then when date night pops up, pick something, and do it! We highly recommend a weekly date night, but remember to take turns planning.

PLACES TO SEE:

- _____
- _____
- _____
- _____
- _____
- _____
- _____
- _____
- _____
- _____
- _____
- _____
- _____
- _____
- _____
- _____

RESTAURANTS TO TRY:

- _____
- _____
- _____
- _____
- _____
- _____
- _____
- _____
- _____
- _____
- _____
- _____
- _____
- _____
- _____
- _____

THINGS TO DO:

- _____
- _____
- _____
- _____
- _____
- _____
- _____
- _____
- _____
- _____
- _____
- _____
- _____
- _____
- _____
- _____

COUPLES TO INVITE OUT:

- _____
- _____
- _____
- _____
- _____
- _____
- _____
- _____
- _____
- _____
- _____
- _____
- _____
- _____
- _____
- _____

At Home Date Night Ideas

1. Plan your dream vacation
2. Play card games
3. Watch a movie & enjoy a themed dinner
4. Have a wine, bread, and cheese night – European style
5. Dance together
6. Do a puzzle
7. Look at your wedding video and pictures
8. Cook a fancy dinner together
9. Read a book together
10. Have your own wine, beer or exotic soda tasting night
11. Sit by your fireplace and chat
12. Camp in your living room
13. Get two canvases and paint together
14. Have a karaoke night
15. Exchange massages or foot rubs
16. Watch old home videos of you and/or your kids
17. Play board games
18. Scavenger Hunt
19. Picnic at home
20. Breakfast in Bed
21. Remake the first dinner out you had together
22. Make freezer meals together
23. Activities that don't involve electricity
24. Virtual tour of a museum
25. Watch a Documentary
26. Make fondue
27. Have an indoor picnic
28. Day Dream together
29. Have a chocolate tasting night
30. Challenge each other in a cooking competition
31. Project a movie in your backyard
32. Workout together
33. Make a spa night
34. Tackle a DIY project
35. Play some video games
36. Stargaze
37. Play a kid's game, like hide and seek
38. Write love letters to each other
39. Practice your spouse's love language
40. Play a video game together
41. Takeout and candlelight
42. Learn something new together
43. Chocolate fondue and fruit over dreaming about your future together
44. Create a seasonal bucket list together
45. Make a goofy video together
46. Phone game competition
47. Design your dream home
48. Nerf Gun War
49. DIY Travel Map
50. Dream together. Where do you want to be in 5 years? 10 years?

Marriage Bucket List

Take a little time to sit down together and dream about the future. What are your big goals? What are your big dreams? Are there things you want to do, places you want to go, people you want to see? (ie: paying off debt, traveling to Italy, seeing a special concert) Write it all down, and include a time frame. As you achieve these goals and make these dreams realities, check each one off!

WHAT DO YOU WANT TO DO?	BY WHEN?	WE DID IT!

Printable Scripture Cards

1 Thessalonians 5:16-18

Rejoice always, pray continually, give thanks in all circumstances; for this is God's will for you in Christ Jesus.

James 1:19

My dear brothers and sisters: You must all be quick to listen, slow to speak, and slow to get angry.

Proverbs 16:24

Kind words are like honey sweet to the soul and healthy for the body.

1 Thessalonians 5:11

So encourage each other and build each other up, just as you are already doing.

Printable Scripture Cards

Hebrews 3:13

But encourage one another daily, as long as it is called "Today," so that none of you may be hardened by sin's deceitfulness.

1 Peter 4:8

Above all, love each other deeply, because love covers over a multitude of sins.

Acts 20:35

It is more blessed to give than to receive.

Romans 12:10

Be devoted to one another in love. Honor one another above yourselves.

Printable Scripture Cards

Ephesians 4:32

Be kind and compassionate to one another, forgiving each other, just as in Christ God forgave you.

Genesis 2:18

The Lord God said, "It is not good for the man to be alone. I will make a helper suitable for him."

John 15:30

My command is this: Love each other as I have loved you.

Ephesians 5:21

Submit to one another out of reverence for Christ.

Acts of Kindness for Your Spouse

Day 1	Day 2	Day 3	Day 4	Day 5	Day 6	Day 7
Leave an unexpected note of appreciation	Get up early and make breakfast for your partner	Clean your spouse's car	Tell your mate something you appreciate about them	Call them unexpectedly during the day just to say "I love you"	Give your spouse a scalp or hand massage	Watch their favorite show with them
Day 8	**Day 9**	**Day 10**	**Day 11**	**Day 12**	**Day 13**	**Day 14**
Arrange for your spouse to have a night out with friends	Surprise your mate with a warm towel after shower	Create a playlist of your spouse's favorite songs or songs from when you were dating	Make a list of all the things you love about your partner and leave it on their pillow	Ask your spouse about their day and listen with interest	Make a sack lunch for your spouse to bring to work	Do one of your spouse's chores
Day 15	**Day 16**	**Day 17**	**Day 18**	**Day 19**	**Day 20**	**Day 21**
Leave a Post-It note with a sweet message on the steering wheel	Tell your spouse something you admire about them	Give your spouse a neck massage	Read a book your spouse has recently read to discuss it	Get dressed up just to greet your spouse at the end of a long day	Surprise your spouse with a small gift "Just because"	Tell them your favorite memory of the two of you together
Day 22	**Day 23**	**Day 24**	**Day 25**	**Day 26**	**Day 27**	**Day 28**
Prepare your spouse's favorite dinner	Text or e-mail your spouse throughout the day	Do their laundry for them	Plan a date or getaway with your spouse	Hide a love note or photograph in your spouse's wallet	Give your spouse a back rub before bed	Help your spouse with a project
Day 29	*Day 30*	*Day 31*				
Print photos of you and your spouse and place them around the bedroom mirror	Give your spouse a hand when they are busy	*Open for you to choose*				

10

Quality Time

Spending "Quality Time" together doesn't have to cost you a lot of money. It is the uninterrupted, focused attention of your loved one that matters.

"Undivided Attention"

1. Make date night a weekly event. Put it on the calendar.
2. Grab some snacks and play a board game.
3. Put away your PHONE!
4. Go on a picnic.
5. Spend 5 minutes in deep conversation before bed.
6. Take a walk together and discuss your future.
7. Go out on the town.
8. Take your lunch break together.
9. Make a coffee shop run together.
10. Go on a bike ride.
11. Volunteer at a non-profit together.
12. Read a book together and talk about it.
13. Do chores together, make it fun.
14. Take trips together.
15. One-on-one conversations.
16. Try a new restaurant.
17. Do a random act of kindness.
18. Do something they want to do.
19. Create a new ritual.
20. Read a book together and talk about it.
21. Don't "listen" while multi-tasking.
22. Use conversation starters to get to know each other better.
23. Take a class together.
24. Talk & connect. No phones, no social media.
25. Camp out in the backyard.
26. Be a kid again! Have fun.
27. Ask, "What was the best part of your day?"
28. Make time together a priority.
29. Look each other in the eyes.
30. Let them know you miss them and can't wait to spend time with them!

QUICK TIPS:
It's not about the amount of time, its more about making the most of the time you do have together! No interrupting and offer empathy not advice.

www.RelentlessMarriage.com

Words of Affirmation A Husband May Want to Hear

1. Thanks for being a great husband!
2. I'm glad you're my friend.
3. You're a great (are going to be a great) Dad!
4. Thanks so much for fixing that!
5. I really appreciate you.
6. You are my man!
7. You are my protector.
8. You are awesome!
9. I respect you so much.
10. Thanks for working so hard.
11. You're an excellent provider.
12. You make me feel like a Lady.
13. I love being with you.
14. You're so smart.
15. You're amazing!
16. Thank you, that was really kind.
17. You're so strong.
18. You're a hard worker.
19. You know how to make me happy!
20. When you hold me tight, I feel safe with you.
21. I love your sense of humor.
22. Thanks for the date . . .
23. Thank you for thinking of me.
24. You're so considerate.
25. You're a great lover.
26. I'll always stand by your side.
27. Your secrets are safe with me.
28. I'm yours.
29. I'm blessed you are my husband.
30. You are a godly man.
31. Thank you for leading our family.
32. You are the first place I turn.
33. It's a lot of fun being Mrs. ( )
34. Your ideas are so exciting!
35. I love how steady and stable you are . . . makes me feel secure.
36. I love it when you barbeque!
37. Thanks for helping around the house.
38. It's fun to work with you.
39. What a great job – that looks fantastic!
40. You are one handsome man.
41. You are an unselfish person.
42. I've learned so much from you.
43. Our kids are fortunate you are their dad.
44. I'm a better woman because you're my husband. I mean that.
45. You are my favorite person in the entire world!
46. I want to grow old with you.
47. You're a great kisser.
48. I'm thinking we should go to bed early tonight . . .
49. You make me feel like a woman.
50. You're a rock.
51. I trust your judgment.
52. Your approval means the world to me.
53. You are a thoughtful man.
54. Thank you for caring how I feel.
55. I appreciate how you show me respect.
56. I have confidence in your leadership.
57. I totally trust you.
58. I'm proud to be your wife.
59. God has my best in mind. That's why he gave me you.
60. There's no one like you.
61. You inspire me to be the best I can be.
62. The hard times don't matter – I'm with you.
63. You stand for the Truth. I admire that.
64. Your enthusiasm gets me excited.
65. You are a man of conviction.
66. I married a man of integrity.
67. You're amazing – you really are!
68. I wouldn't trade my life with you for anything.
69. You're a man of action.
70. You're my dream-come-true.
71. I will always be loyal to you.
72. No other man could even come close.
73. You will always have my heart.
74. There's no one like you.
75. What do you need from me?
76. I am one blessed woman!
77. I love being by your side.
78. You look great!
79. You were amazing last night.
80. I'm always in your corner.
81. You helped me to become a better woman.
82. You have a lot to offer.
83. Thank you for being a faithful husband.
84. Being with you is my favorite place to be.
85. Our kids really look up to you . . . and so do I.
86. Do you know how much I love you?
87. You're a gentleman.
88. I love just being with you.
89. I'll love you always and forever.
90. Thank you for listening.

Words of Affirmation A Wife May Want to Hear

1. You give a lot, I appreciate how much you give.
2. You are beautiful.
3. You make me want to be a better man.
4. Thanks for your faithfulness to our family.
5. You are a godly woman.
6. I've learned a lot from you.
7. I've seen you grow so much.
8. I like spending time with you.
9. You're fun to be with.
10. What a fantastic meal!
11. You make wonderful things.
12. Thanks for your diligence in running this house.
13. Our kids are fortunate to have you as their mom.
14. God wants me happy... He made you my wife.
15. You bring out the best in me.
16. You are a fantastic person.
17. You are deep and thoughtful.
18. You're as beautiful to me as the day we married.
19. My favorite place to be is with you.
20. I wouldn't be half the man I am without you.
21. You make loving fun.
22. You compliment me as a wife.
23. You are my world.
24. The Bible tells men: Love your wife like Christ loves the Church . . . I like my job!
25. I like going out with you . . . busy tonight?
26. You are a hard worker.
27. You're so smart.
28. I value your insight.
29. You have a lot to offer.
30. I really admire your inner strength
31. I'm glad our kids have (will have) such an excellent role model.
32. You are (will be) an amazing mother.
33. You know you're my best friend, don't you?
34. I don't know what I would do without you.
35. You make me a happy man.
36. I'm amazed at the women you've become.
37. You accomplish a lot.
38. You are so thoughtful.
39. Thank you for respecting me.
40. I'm grateful I can trust you with anything.
41. I have total confidence in you.
42. I'm proud to be your husband.
43. God knew what I needed. That's why He brought us together.
44. I respect the woman you are.
45. I appreciate your wisdom.
46. I rely on your discernment.
47. I appreciate all your efforts.
48. You've got great ideas.
49. I married up!
50. I appreciate your intuition.
51. You're the finest woman on the planet!
52. I can face anything with you by my side.
53. I married a winner!
54. Our kids love you so much.
55. You are the best woman I know.
56. I don't deserve you . . . I'm glad you're mine!
57. I want to grow old with you.
58. Thank you for being so good to me.
59. You're an awesome lover.
60. I don't need anything else – just you.
61. I only have eyes for you.
62. I'll always be faithful to you.
63. You never have to wonder where I am.
64. Thank you for standing by me.
65. I really appreciate your loyalty.
66. You are a great cook/chef.
67. You're so creative.
68. I love what you make.
69. You are one talented woman!
70. You never stop giving.
71. You look fabulous in that outfit!
72. You make me look good!
73. When you walked into the room, you took my breath away.
74. You are an excellent wife.
75. You bring me joy.
76. I love the home that you've created.
77. You work hard to make things wonderful.
78. The Song of Solomon has nothing on you!
79. I'm a better man because of you.
80. You are a unique person.
81. I'm glad I married you!
82. You'll always have my heart.
83. Your heart is safe with me.
84. I'll love you forever.
85. You are God's perfect choice for me.
86. I wouldn't want any other life than the one I am living with you.
87. You are my dream girl.
88. You are a beautiful person, inside and out.
89. You impress me, you really do!
90. You are a woman of integrity.

Physical Affection

PHYSICAL AFFECTION

35 WAYS TO SHOW YOUR LOVED ONE PHYSICAL TOUCH

1. A sweet hug
2. Hold their hands
3. Pat their back
4. Rub their shoulders
5. Give them a foot rub
6. Put your hand in the small of her back
7. Hold her head when you hug her
8. Kiss her forehead
9. Kiss her cheek

10. Rub his shoulder when he is tense
11. Cuddle on the couch
12. For your kiddos…snuggle for story time
13. Play footsies
14. For your kids...have a secret handshake
15. Hug each other for no reason

16. Touch foreheads
17. Kiss his neck
18. Rub his back
19. Put your arm around her waist
20. Give him a massage
21. Tickle his knee
22. Rest your head on his shoulder
23. Hold hands when you walk together
24. For the kiddos...tickle fights!
25. A high five
26. Sit close as you watch TV together

27. Stroke his hair as you give him a compliment
28. Hold hands while watching a movie together
29. Sit close at dinner
30. Touch his forearm when you speak
31. Rub his leg
32. Hold his face in hands
33. Stare into the eyes
34. Squeeze his hands at an inside joke you have together
35. Give him a bear hug

PHYSICAL AFFECTION DOES INCLUDE SEXUAL INTIMACY FOR MARRIED COUPLES. IT ALSO CAN INCLUDE SIMPLE, NON-SEXUAL TOUCHES THAT CAN MAKE OUR LOVED ONES FEEL LOVED.

Receiving Gifts

Receiving Gifts

1. Make even an average day as exciting as a holiday
2. Buy your spouse lunch and bring it to work
3. Have they casually mentioned how much they love something? Pick it up for them, and surprise them any given day
4. Don't just bless them with a gift on their birthday or Christmas
5. Create something special. A homemade gift sometimes means more than store-bought
6. Pick them up a card at the store
7. Have fresh flowers on the table when they get home
8. Make them a scrapbook of your photos together
9. Create a journal of special memories you share
10. Bring something tangible home from vacation
11. Pick up a special treat for them at the grocery store

12. Surprise your loved one with a little gift on their vehicle in the morning or after work
13. Take them out on a date and have a gift waiting at the table
14. Give them the gift of time. Give them you...
15. Do not forget their birthday, anniversary, or special dates
16. Give with your whole heart
17. Purchase a book they have wanted
18. Give them a gift certificate for a car wash
19. Put their favorite quote or Bible Verse in a frame as a special gift
20. Frame a special date you share "Our Friendship Est. 2010" for example
21. When you are at the store with your child, but them a small pack of gum at the check out
22. Have flowers sent to your loved one for no reason

27 WAYS TO BLESS THOSE WHO FEEL LOVED RECEIVING GIFTS

23. Pick them a wildflower
24. Put together a book of quotes or phrases that remind you of them
25. Buy them a new DVD that you can watch together
26. Drop a small gift to them at work
27. Take them out to their favorite place

GIVING GIFTS TO YOUR LOVED ONES DOES
NOT HAVE TO BREAK THE BANK.
IN FACT, SOMETIMES THE SMALLEST, MOST
INEXPENSIVE GIFTS WHEN GIVEN WITH A LOVING
HEART MEAN THE MOST

Replacing Thoughts

How to Stop Negative Self Talk with Scripture

When you hear/feel/think:	Replace it with:
I am invisible.	I have been established, anointed, and sealed by God! -2 Corinthians 1:21-22
I am nothing special.	I am God's workmanship! -Ephesians 2:10
I am not good enough.	I have been chosen and God desires me to bear fruit. -John 15:1,5
I'll never accomplish anything worthwhile.	I have a purpose! -Ephesians 1:9
I might as well give up in defeat.	I am victorious! -1 John 5:4
I am too broken and distraught to go on.	I have a heart and mind that is protected with God's peace. - Philippians 4:7
I have been rejected again.	I am chosen and dearly loved. - Colossians 3:12
I am unforgivable.	I am blameless. -1 Corinthians 1:8
I am stuck in this unhealthy place.	I am set free! - Romans 8:2, John 8:32
I cannot let go of my past.	I have been redeemed! - Isaiah 44:22

Confident People vs Insecure People

NEW NATURE   **VS.**   **OLD NATURE**

CONFIDENT PEOPLE   **VS.**   **INSECURE PEOPLE**

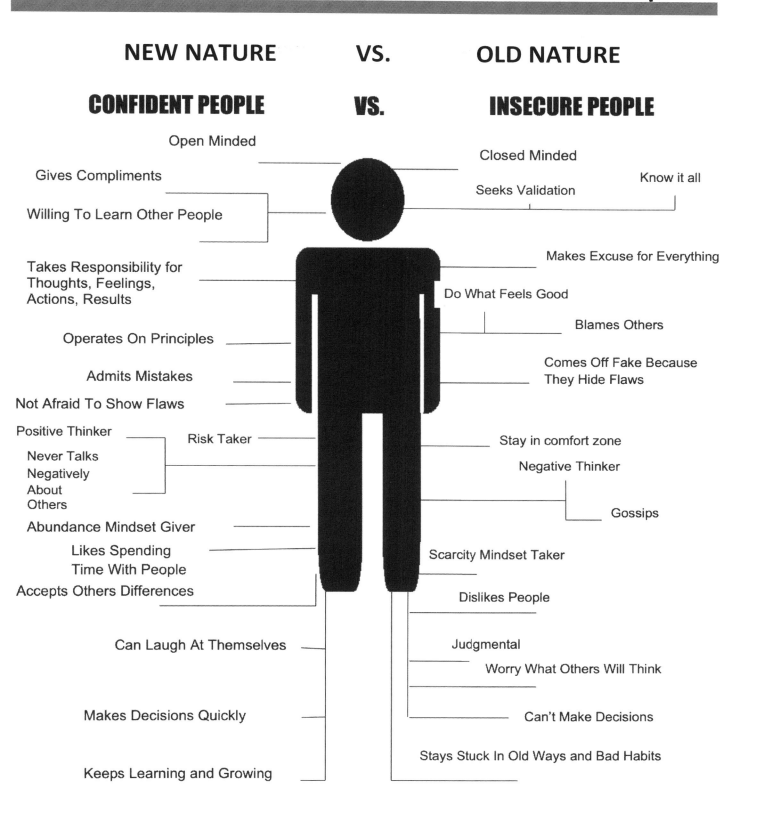

Confident People (left):
- Open Minded
- Gives Compliments
- Willing To Learn Other People
- Takes Responsibility for Thoughts, Feelings, Actions, Results
- Operates On Principles
- Admits Mistakes
- Not Afraid To Show Flaws
- Positive Thinker
- Risk Taker
- Never Talks Negatively About Others
- Abundance Mindset Giver
- Likes Spending Time With People
- Accepts Others Differences
- Can Laugh At Themselves
- Makes Decisions Quickly
- Keeps Learning and Growing

Insecure People (right):
- Closed Minded
- Know it all
- Seeks Validation
- Makes Excuse for Everything
- Do What Feels Good
- Blames Others
- Comes Off Fake Because They Hide Flaws
- Stay in comfort zone
- Negative Thinker
- Gossips
- Scarcity Mindset Taker
- Dislikes People
- Judgmental
- Worry What Others Will Think
- Can't Make Decisions
- Stays Stuck In Old Ways and Bad Habits

17

Responding Rather than Reacting

Responding Rather than Reacting to Your Partner

- As you notice yourself reacting with words or strong urges to speak, disagree, explain yourself, etc., take 6 deep, slow belly breaths, and it does not count if you do this to attract attention. You are doing this to soothe and calm yourself so that you can listen to your partner's perspective. The only way the two of you can have a healthy relationship is by knowing how you each see things differently. Your goal is to be two separate and equal people who are speaking, sharing and earnestly working to understand two different points of view.

- When your partner has finished speaking, to be certain you have understood what was said, STATE THE OBVIOUS, and remember to VALIDATE.

  For example, "You are really mad. It's hard for me to listen, I want to defend myself, but I will calm myself and respect what you have to say."

  Stating what is obvious about your partner, and real for you helps you to calm yourself and gives you an opportunity to switch from reacting to responding, thus engaging your thoughts and feelings while putting your needs, thoughts and feelings second to your partner who is speaking and sharing. You can wait for your turn. Waiting is an act of personal and relationship respect as well as an act of maturity.

- Then as you calm and push yourself to stay focused on what your partner is saying, ask him/her TWO questions. These are questions designed to objectively and empathetically learn more about what your partner is feeling, thinking and needing. These questions are genuine and designed to help your partner really share and describe his/her feelings.

  For example, "How long have you been angry with me about this?" or "What first made you angry?" and "Do you have other feelings about this?"

  Each time you practice this new set of behaviors you will find this becomes easier and that you are able to remain in the conversations longer and to a more productive end.

- REMEMBER: It's not about me! S/he and I are separate people and I must listen to what is important to my partner. S/he is describing and sharing her/his experience. We are different people with different viewpoints.

7 Keys to Better Love

It won't take you long to notice this is a little more than a checklist. In addition to actionable steps that you can take, we've also included some nuggets of truth that have impacted our hearts, and we hope will impact yours as well. There are prayer prompts and more. May the Lord bless all of your effort in your marriage, and be the source of victorious, life changing love in you.

1 Corinthians 13:4-8 (NKJV)

4 *Love suffers long and is kind; love does not envy; love does not parade itself, is not puffed up;* **5** *does not behave rudely, does not seek its own, is not provoked, thinks no evil;* **6** *does not rejoice in iniquity, but rejoices in the truth;* **7** *bears all things, believes all things, hopes all things, endures all things.* **8** *Love never fails. But whether there are prophecies, they will fail; whether there are tongues, they will cease; whether there is knowledge, it will vanish away.*

This passage is not exclusive to marriage. The love described there is to be universal to all believers, and practiced in all the relationships of all believers, married or not. It should not be taken out of context to mean that you are stuck in a marriage with abuse, persistent unfaithfulness, or an unsaved spouse who wants out. That is not the intent of these verses, as the context has to do with the body of Christ as a whole, and doesn't actually even mention the marriage relationship. If you are being hurt, find a safe place and get help.

1. Love is patient, love is kind and is not jealous

Did you know that the golden rule existed long before Jesus spoke it? Interestingly, it existed in the negative form. "Don't do to others what you wouldn't want done to you." When Jesus spoke it, He turned it to a positive. *An action, not merely a restraint from action.* This type of kindness is an action that requires the help of the Spirit to live out.

"But the fruit of the Spirit is love, joy, peace, longsuffering, kindness, goodness, faithfulness, gentleness, self-control. Against such there is no law." **Galatians 5:22-23, NKJV**

Kindness, patience, and love itself, are fruits of the Spirit. They spring from His love in us, and His kindness and patience toward us. Lack of patience reveals a weak spot in our love. Name a way you can show supernatural kindness, and a way to show supernatural patience toward your spouse. Then pray for God's help to accomplish it.

○ _____   ○ _____

Not all jealousy is bad. There are some situations in which jealousy is right and appropriate. *The jealousy spoken of in this verse however, is envy.* The sinful kind of jealousy. If you compare your spouse to others or your marriage to others, then it's time to pray.

- ○ Ask for forgiveness for comparisons, and help to replace this habit with thankfulness
- ○ Pray that God will show you verses to cling to that will help you know how to be content
- ○ Pray also that He will give you verses that will direct you in how to build up your marriage

2. Love does not brag and is not arrogant, does not act unbecomingly

"Therefore, let him who thinks he stands take heed lest he fall." *1 Corinthians 10:12 NKJV*

- Practice crowding out pride and false humility by focusing on the Almighty God and your complete reliance on Him.
- Spend some time singing praise to Him today.
- Let that place of worship dictate your attitude. If you feel the temptation to be rude or prideful, go back to the place of worship in your heart.
- Pray. Refocus. Repeat.

3. Love does not seek its own, it is not easily provoked

This simple little phrase is aimed right at the core of human selfishness. True love puts the needs of others before our own. That doesn't mean that we wear ourselves out, becoming martyrs on the altar of our spouse's comfort. It does mean that we care for each other and seek what is truly best for each other, physically and spiritually. Always seek each other's best. We also practice responding in love rather than reacting in provocation.

What are you holding onto that is not in the best interest of your spouse or your marriage?

- _____

How can you change this?

- _____

- Pray for God to help you love so much that you are not provoked. The irritant may remain, but the response can change.

Find a scripture that will help you respond in love rather than aggravation, and memorize it.

- _____

4. Does not take into account a wrong suffered

The further we go into this glorious description of love, the more we are pressed to acknowledge that we cannot attain it in our own power. When tensions rise, do you feel past offenses flooding in, teaming up with the current wrong? Does today's frustration get added to an ever-growing list of ways your spouse is not measuring up?

- Pray that God will help you forgive past hurts, and help you wholeheartedly love your spouse, accepting them just as they are. Deal with one issue at a time, and don't bring last year's issues into today's interactions. Period.

5. Love does not rejoice in unrighteousness, but rejoices with the truth

"Do not let kindness and truth leave you." *Proverbs 3:3a NASB*

How is the truth used in your marriage? Is it wielded as a weapon of war? Is it suppressed for the sake of peace? Is it ignored or skirted around? To rejoice in truth, and not unrighteousness, requires that love be our motivation. Shooting truth bombs at each other to win a fight isn't loving. Avoiding truth for our own comfort is dishonest.

Jesus knew all there was to know about every sinner he encountered. He only ever spoke truth, and His truth brought life to his people, not further shame, hurt, or guilt. He didn't ignore sin, but neither did He shame the sinner. Follow Jesus' example in your communication today, and speak life giving truth to your spouse.

❍ Find encouraging truths from scripture to share with your spouse when they are discouraged. List them below for quick reference.

_____

_____

_____

Name some things your spouse has done well. Share these with them randomly.

❍ _____

❍ _____

❍ _____

6. Love bears all things, believes all things, hopes all things, endures all things

In a marriage of *two God-fearing believers,* this love should be practiced. That means, there are no concerns of being married to the wrong person. Divorce is not discussed, joked about, or secretly considered. *There are certain situations that call for separation or even divorce, but the heart is always for love, redemption, reconciliation, and faithfulness. In such cases, seek Godly counselors and therapists as needed to work through the issues.*

❍ Spend 15 minutes in prayer today for your marriage. Pray that you will both be able to bear all, believe all, hope all, and endure all.

❍ Pray specifically and humbly, because your marriage is made up of two sinners.

❍ Ask God to bring scriptures to your mind as you need them, and the right resources to your hands too. Then go seek them out.

7. Love never fails

While 1 Corinthians 13 does not exclusively apply to marriage, we believe that in the context of marriage, it applies to every part of the relationship including sex. Do not let it end.

I can't address all the problems that arise in a sexual relationship in this space, but here's a start.

> ➤ Pain: Sex shouldn't hurt and if it does, it's usually a treatable issue, so see a doctor about pain.

> ➤ Emotional disconnect: We recommend, "How We Love", by Milan and Kay Yerkovich, if you want to build your emotional connection.

> ➤ Stress: Stress needs to be managed.

> ➤ Pleasure: Both partners pleasure is necessary.

What is your biggest challenge or frustration in your sexual relationship? What can you do today to work toward a solution?

O _____

_____

What is your spouse's biggest challenge or frustration in your sexual relationship? What can you do today to work toward a solution?

O _____

_____

Research. Be kind. Be merciful to each other. Work on yourself, not your spouse. Love your spouse through all their failures. If love has shown signs of ending, seek further therapy/counseling. Love on.

If you have questions or thoughts, please reach out to us at info@MyMarriageIntensive.com. We love to hear from you, and read all of your emails!

How to Show Your Spouse Respect

Respect is vital to a connected marriage. Several ways to show respect is by listening to your spouse's opinions, asking for their help, letting them lead, initiating sex, and learning to admire and appreciate each other.

Respect is a core pillar and an absolutely necessary element of a good marriage. Here are a few ways to show your spouse respect.

1. **Accept that you married an imperfect person**

We all make mistakes and nobody is perfect. Your spouse knows he or she will make mistakes, but what lifts them up is knowing that you support them and will still stand by them no matter what.

2. **Focus on what your spouse does well**

Look for ways to build up your spouse by encouraging them in what they do well. As their spouse, you see things in them that they don't in themselves.

3. **Protect your marriage reputation**

You don't want to give your spouse any doubt that you don't have their back. What you say about your spouse in front of others shows how much you respect your spouse. If you're gossiping and venting about what your spouse has done to frustrate you, it may feel good to be consoled by others but you're actually hurting your marriage and your spouse.

4. **Give them space**

Sometimes we as an individual need some alone time to gather our thoughts and collect ourselves. Giving your spouse space until they're ready allows them to be in the right mind and able to make the best decisions for both of you. Everyone has different ways of relieving stress.

5. **Be present and in the moment**

Especially when resolving conflict. Keep your head in the conversation and pay attention. Respect your spouse by listening to them when they talk to you. Keep eye contact and put away any distractions.

6. **Pay attention to each other's physical and emotional needs**

Physical intimacy strengthens a marriage. It's a bond that should only be between husband and wife. If your spouse is in need of intimacy (including emotional), you are the person best suited to fulfill that need.

7. **Be forgiving of mistakes**

Similar to #1, your spouse is imperfect and will make mistakes. When you forgive your spouse for something they've done you allow them to start over and rebuild trust.

How to Create Emotional Safety in Marriage

There are 9 attitudes that will help build emotional safety in your marriage. As we cultivate these attitudes (which should result in similar behavior and actions) we will create a climate of emotional security, freedom and connection.

These attitudes are keys that open your marriage to its true potential AND locks the doors to thieves that steal your emotional security.

They are in no particular order.

#1 Kindness

Never underestimate the power of simple kindness. There is something powerful and meaningful about kindness. It doesn't take a lot of effort to express kindness. Compassion creates a bond that connects us to others.

Kindness binds us together.

And when it comes to marriage, kindness is one of the most important 'acts' that connects us.

As John Gottman says: *"Kindness glues couples together."*

Other research validates this. It is the most important predictor of satisfaction and stability in a relationship.

The reason?

When we express kindness, we are saying, 'You matter to me!' It creates an atmosphere where our partner feels understood, validated and loved. Kindness says, "I care."

One Important Aspect

I've heard couples say, "Well, that sounds good, but that's just not how we are. I'm not kind by nature." That's a fallacy. It's an excuse. And quite frankly, if your marriage matters to you, change your perspective.

Kindness, as well as any character trait, is **something we must develop. It's like a muscle.** The more you use it, the stronger it becomes.

Sure, some people are naturally more kind than others. But that cannot be used as an excuse to refuse to grow in kindness.

Here's a Key

It's tough to extend kindness during a heated argument. When tempers are flared (red zone) and you feel misunderstood, it's difficult to 'think about being kind.'

That's why you need to practice when things are going well. The more you cultivate the habit of being nice (kind), the easier it will be when things are tough.

#2 Respect

Fill in the blank:

I feel respected when _____.

Think about it before you answer. Respect is one of the key building blocks of a successful marriage.

What exactly is respect?

Look up the definition and you'll find something like this:

1. a feeling of deep admiration for someone or something elicited by their abilities, qualities, or achievements.
2. due regard for the feelings, wishes, rights, or traditions of others.

The core of respect is treating each other well.

"When you and your partner care about each other's feelings, you'll go out of your way to take care of each other to make each other feel emotionally safe."

Emotional security is **connected to mutual respect.**

We will not always agree, but we must value each other enough to listen and work toward common ground.

"In an emotionally safe marriage each spouse feels valued, understood, and accepted. They may not always agree with each other, but each partner attempts to understand the other's point of view with warmth and empathy. In these solid marriages spouses are not afraid to radically disagree because they know that afterward they have the capacity to emotionally reconnect."

Pillars of a Healthy Respect

There are three pillars of a successful marriage. Integrity, respect and endurance. (Remember our foundation is on God).

Trust is based upon respect. And respect is built upon trust. It's difficult to respect (hold in high esteem) something you do not trust. The fact that you do not trust indicates you do not esteem it.

Practical Steps to Build Respect

There are simple things you can do to create an environment of respect.

1. Never Speak Down to Your Spouse
2. Keep Your Word
3. Sincerely Value Their Opinion
4. Create Clear Boundaries
5. Discuss Your Differences

Men and women often define love differently. Neither seems to be able to clearly define respect. That's why I asked you to fill in the blank above. It's important to **discuss what respect means** (and doesn't mean) in your marriage.

As we talk about these issues, we **come closer to understanding how they fit into our relationship**.

Side Note: One of the ways to build respect in your marriage is to work together to create a **'marriage mission statement.'** Couples who believe they are together for a purpose are happier, healthier and have greater respect for each other. They work together instead of working separate from one another.

#3 Appreciation

"As we express our gratitude, we must never forget that the highest appreciation is not to utter words, but to live by them."
John F. Kennedy

When we think of appreciation, we usually think of gratitude. Like the quote above. But appreciation has a much deeper meaning.

Think of it this way. We use the term appreciation **when we talk about the value of our home increasing**. We say "Our home appreciated in value."

In contrast, we use depreciation when the value of something goes down.

Think of appreciation in your marriage as the actions you take to bring increased value to the relationship.

Two Types of People

John Gottman talks about two types of people. He calls them the "masters" and the "disasters."

Masters are positive. **Disasters** are negative.

But it runs deeper than that. He explains:

"There's a habit of mind that the masters have, which is this: they are scanning social environment for things they can appreciate and say thank you for. They are building this culture of respect and appreciation very purposefully. Disasters are scanning the social environment for partners' mistakes."

In essence, disaster people are not adding value. They are depreciating their spouse.

Julie Gottman adds:

"It's not just scanning environment. It's scanning the partner for what the partner is doing right or scanning him for what he's doing wrong and criticizing versus respecting him and expressing appreciation."

Appreciation indicates the value we place on our spouse.

Read that again slowly. It's true.

If you value your spouse, you will show appreciation. Where there is little appreciation, there is little trust. **Without trust, you cannot build a bridge of love.**

When I am thankful, I acknowledge the value that's been added to my life.

It also has a positive impact on our emotions. The more thankful we are, the better we feel.

As Gottman relates, **when we look for the value of our spouse, we are more likely to express gratitude.** This in turn causes the value of our relationship to increase.

#4 Affirmation

Here's a powerful statement I want you to think about:

Be a cheerleader; not a coach.

We often think we are doing good when we try to coach our spouse into being better. In reality, this usually has the opposite effect. Instead of doing better, they interpret this as not measuring up.

Don't get me wrong, there is a time and place for coaching. But rarely should this happen between spouses.

That's not to say we can't correct, discuss, challenge or disagree. All of these are legitimate and healthy.

But...Primarily we should **seek to affirm our spouse.** When this becomes the norm in a relationship, health always follows.

The Habit of Speaking Well

One of the reasons people have a great marriage is it is built on affirmation. These couples have **a strong habit of speaking well of each other,** and saying publicly how great our spouse is.

The Power of Affirmation

There are many psychological studies that verify how powerful our affirmations are. I think this happens for a couple of reasons:

1. It keeps us focused on the positive (What you appreciate, appreciates).

It's easy to get negative if we don't consciously focus on the positive. When we speak positive, the mind thinks positive.

2. It trains the brain to think of the good.

Our thoughts are generally the result of what we have trained our mind to think about. Our minds get in a rut. Whether good or bad.

Some scientists even believe there are literal "grooves in the brain" when we think on a subject over an extended period of time.

"We don't see things as they are, we see things as we are".

That's why it is important to guard our thoughts, words and actions. Make sure we are acting in sync with our goals. In this case, the goal is to create a marriage built on emotional safety.

#5 Being Mindful

Being mindful is about focus. Giving attention to the relationship.

Because our lives are usually run at break-neck speed, we have to consciously decide to slow down and give attention to the things that matter.

Let's face it, we all get caught up in the rat race from time to time. But if we value our relationship, we will invest time, energy and attention to make it better. This is mindfulness. Concentrated time, energy and attention.

Know Where You Are at Any Given Moment

We need to make it a practice to know where we are in our marriage at any given moment. This is why it's important to take stock. Evaluate.

Quick Illustration:

It's like the big map at a theme park. If you want to know how to get to the giant water slide, you need to know where you currently are located. Then, and only then, can you navigate the place you want to be.

Same with marriage. If you aren't sure where you are in your relationship, it's virtually impossible to get to where you want to be.

Occasionally couples stumble into a great relationship; yet even then, they have other factors (principles) in place that make it easy for them to make it. It seems like an accidental discovery, in reality they had key things in place that helped them get there.

How to Practice Mindfulness

Practicing mindfulness is simply being present.

Here's a few things you can do to make it a habit:

1. Set Aside Time

Most people spell love T.I.M.E.

It's impossible to be present (mindful) if you are not present (there).

2. Keep a Gratitude Journal

Journaling is a great way to monitor your spiritual and mental life. It's also an excellent way to focus on the things that matter.

I've often encouraged couples to keep a gratitude journal to record the positive things about your marriage.

It's a great way to force yourself to stay focused on the good things about your relationship. What you continually focus on becomes more pronounced in your life.

In other words, i**f you focus on good things, you will see more good things.** However, if you choose to see the negative, you will find it easier to see more negative. It's true that you usually *find what you are looking for*. So, look for the best.

A gratitude journal helps build the habit of "**good consciousness**" or benefit of the doubt.

3. Tell Them

Not only record the positive things about your relationship, but tell your spouse about those good things. Share your relationship wins with each other.

The more you say it, the more real it becomes. That's why you should conscientiously and consistently tell your spouse how much you value them.

4. Turn Off Distractions

The biggest thief of mindfulness is the **little things that beg for our attention.** The cell phone. Social media. Television.

Make it a habit of turning off distractions.

#6 Open Communication

Open, deep and meaningful conversation builds a heart connection that is strong and formidable. There is something about being open and transparent (add to this accepted and valued) that makes us bond on an emotional level.

However, many couples have the wrong idea about communication.

Communication is not:

1. Proving Your Point.

The drive to 'be right' all the time will destroy your effectiveness in communicating.

Yes. There are times issues need to be hashed out and facts are important. But many couples reduce communicating to simply trying to get their point across.

2. Saying Things Louder to Be Heard.

We often think that yelling will help get our point across. The opposite is true.

A recent study measured how well people remembered information that was delivered with different emotions.

Their analyses showed that participants recognized words better when they had previously heard them in the neutral tone compared with the sad tone. In addition, words were remembered more negatively if they had previously been heard in a sad voice.

In other words, **yelling, crying and heightened emotions did not increase how well they received the information,** it actually hurt it.

3. Selling (convincing) to Get Your Way

There is a sales adage that says: Everyone likes to buy. But nobody likes to be sold.

Selling (in this case) is manipulation.

There are times we need to discuss and decide on a course of action.

We "sell" when we manipulate to get our way. Selling always results in one partner **feeling controlled, dictated and overlooked.**

It never takes into consideration the feelings, desires and wants of your spouse. And it always leaves the relationship suffering.

4. Waiting Until You Are Angry to Talk

Depending on personality type, we deal with problems in one of three ways:

a) We run headlong into battle.
b) We flee to safer ground and avoid.
c) We wait for the right time to discuss the issue.

Obviously the third response is best.

Too often we wait until things are so bad that it is explosive. At that point, the gloves come off and it's a brawl. (Think RED ZONE)

Arguing is not communicating.

Remember the goal of communication is not just the transmission of information; it is connecting with our spouse and entering their world.

5. Using Should and Shouldn't

Let's be honest, when someone TELLS us what we should have done, it rarely sits right.

It comes across bossy and condescending. Avoid using absolute terms like this. It will help you have a more open dialog and move toward a positive relationship.

Open communication is built on the foundation of trust. Without it, it's impossible to connect on a deep level.

#7 Responsibility

"The greatest day in your life and mine is when we take total responsibility for our attitudes. That's the day we truly grow up."
John Maxwell

Emotional security stands on the foundation of personal responsibility.

Taking responsibility for yourself

To feel safe with another person, **you first have to feel safe with yourself**. I'm not talking about the fear you will harm yourself. If this is something you struggle with, please seek professional help immediately. Your life is valuable. Self-harm is destructive on a number of levels. It never accomplishes what is intended.

Feeling safe with yourself has to do with self-acceptance. Loving yourself.

Truth is, **you can't love someone else if you don't love yourself.** Not the self-centered, narcissistic, ego-manic type self-love. The self-love that accepts who you are and how you are. We often call it self-esteem. The fact that you esteem yourself as worthy to be treated good, right and with respect.

If this is missing in you, you will never find it in another person.

The beginning place of a healthy relationship is a healthy individual. This is why fixing another person never works. Only they can fix their life. Sure, they may need help, but **no one can make a decision for you**. You have to take responsibility for your own life.

Taking responsibility for your role in the relationship

You are not responsible for your spouse's self-esteem; only they can create that. You are, however, **responsible to validate it** and let them know they are valued, loved unconditionally, and accepted without reservation.

Why Taking Responsibility Matters

"If you want to be successful, you have to take 100% responsibility for everything that you experience in your life" Jack Canfield.

Until you take responsibility for your life, you are powerless to change it. This is why taking responsibility matters.

If you are NOT responsible, you have no authority or power to make the situation different. You are stuck. Left to the whim of others to make things better.

If you blame your circumstances on others, you are empowering THEM to control your life. THEY have to do something for things to change. So you lose control.

If, however, **you take responsibility, you gain control.**

For example, if your marriage is not what you want it to be, taking responsibility gives you the power to do something about it. It's important to know, responsibility doesn't necessarily mean blame. Just because you take responsibility doesn't mean you take blame. That's important.

Placing blame rarely brings about change anyway.

Taking responsibility means you believe something can be done about the situation, and you have the power to do it.

As long as you blame someone else – your job, your spouse, the kids, hormones, etc. – you put yourself in a place of powerlessness. **Whoever is to blame is the only one who can change things.**

So, take responsibility for what you want your life to be...what you want your marriage to be...and do something about it.

This is the first step toward true freedom.

#8 Releasing

One of my mentors taught me the value of letting go. We all have baggage in our life. Learning to let go of it helps us find freedom.

Unfortunately, our past often controls us.

Let's relate this to marriage. Creating a healthy relationship has two components:

1. Things you bring INTO your marriage...

Things like right attitudes, beliefs, and behaviors. Some of the things we've discussed fall into this category.

We must BRING these things into our relationship if we want a healthy marriage.

2. Things you release FROM your marriage.

These things are equally (sometimes more) important than what you put into your relationship. Many times, it's the things left out that destroy.

Many times, we let little things in our relationship that might seem undetectable. They are small. Yet profoundly significant. Ultimately, they undermine the purity of our marriage.

How to Create Emotional Safety in Marriage (Cont.)

Things That Damage Emotional Safety

There are four things that will destroy emotional safety.

1. Criticism
2. Contempt
3. Defensiveness
4. Stonewalling (walking away from a difficult situation as to not deal with it and shut it out)

Brené Brown reminds us: "Vulnerability is the birthplace of love, belonging, joy, courage, empathy, accountability, and authenticity."

#9 Availability

Two aspects of being available.

First, is making your marriage a priority.

We prioritize by making time.

Think about it. We make time for work. Special events. Even vacations. Why not our marriage?

Don't misunderstand:

Making your relationship a priority is **more than putting an important event on the calendar**. It's about how you **internalize** your relationship.

Is this the most important relationship in your life?

It should be. Needs to be.

If so, then treat it like it is.

Now you can put things on the calendar. But don't confuse scheduling time with your spouse with valuing them as a person.

Second, is making sure you are emotionally accessible.

This is the essence of 'being available.' Being there.

"Why are men so detached?"

I hear that question a lot. Truth is, they are not.

Let me clarify. Most men aren't detached. They may be unlearned. Unskilled in intimacy. Maybe even unsure of themselves. But deep down, I believe (at least my experience indicates this is true) most men want to have a deeply loving relationship with their wife.

Sure, men are wired different.

But we all desire intimacy.

To have intimacy we must be present for our spouse.

We make ourselves known to one another by sharing who we are (our feelings, reactions, values, ideas, fears) and by being open and receptive to our partner's sharing. Couples often report feeling painfully alone when emotional distance becomes the norm.

Finding intimacy begins with discovering ourselves…We have to be visible before we can be seen. We have to be available before our hearts can be affected. And we have to be present before we can be intimate.

Being available is key to creating security in our relationship.

Wrapping It Up

Emotional safety is important for a healthy marriage. Creating a climate for a secure relationship should be top priority.

How to Create Emotional Safety in Marriage (Cont.)

Summary

Here's the 9 keys to creating emotional safety in your marriage.

- #1 Kindness
- #2 Respect
- #3 Appreciation
- #4 Affirmation
- #5 Being Mindful
- #6 Open Communication
- #7 Responsibility
- #8 Releasing
- #9 Availability

Questions

If you were to rate emotional safety in your relationship, what number would you give it [scale of 1-10. 10 being incredibly secure]?

_____

_____

How can your marriage improve in this area?

_____

_____

What steps should you take to create a strong sense of emotional safety with your spouse?

_____

_____

Deepen Intimacy! Practical Tips to Build Closeness

These tips aren't about trying new positions, potions and lotions. Those things are good too, but this is about making real life changes that actually make a difference in the way things go for you both. It is our hope that you and your spouse will work together through this list and make lasting change together, because marriage is teamwork. Relationship and sex are teamwork. Do the work as a team, and reap the fun rewards together.

1. Destress
Brainstorm ways to reduce, and/or manage stress. Easier said than done, I know, but stress is the number one killer of libido for most people, so this is important.

2. Lighten Up
Both of you may need to take everything a little less seriously. Purposefully enjoy life. Enjoy each other, and even appreciate the differences between you.

3. Exercise – Together if Possible
Exercise promotes a sense of well-being. Exercising together makes your brain associate that sense of well-being with your time together. It all happens on a biological level.

4. Stop Chasing Orgasm
Female orgasm plays hard-to-catch. As soon as you try, it runs away. Relax, enjoy the sensations, and just let it happen or not happen.

5. See a Doctor If It Hurts
Occasional discomfort can happen, as with any activity. Consistent pain during sex is not normal, but it is usually treatable. Don't wait. Make an appointment.

6. Turn Off TV and Technology Earlier in the Evening
Give yourself time to come down off the artificial dopamine highs of technology. Take time in the evening to connect with each other. Less blue light also improves sleep.

7. Work Together to Get the Kids to Bed
It takes most of us a solid half hour to unwind after the last "MAMA!!!" of the night. Working together makes that last call happen earlier.

8. Keep Your Room Clean
A clean room helps calm your mind and allows you to focus on each other.

9. Eat for a Healthy Brain and Body
What we eat affects how well we think. Not to mention how our body feels and functions. Research what foods and supplements would help you be at your best. Talk with your doctor before changing diet or adding supplements.

10. Learn About Sex
Learn what God thinks about it, develop a right perspective, and learn tips from reputable sources.

11. Prayer
God cares about your marriage, and your intimacy. Bathe them in prayer.

12. No Pressure, No Accusation, Only Encouragement
Pressure is a turn off. Accusation hurts and is counterproductive. Encouragement promotes healing and growth.

13. Understand that All Desire is "Responsive" and Requires Stimuli
People with "lower drives" require more/stronger stimuli than "higher drives," in order to be turned on. Neither is wrong, just different. Work with the system you have.

14. Communicate What You Like and Don't Care For
Don't expect mind reading. Learn to communicate. A code may help, like three peppers is really spicy, one pepper is a little bland.

15. Be Gracious
We are all imperfect. God is gracious to us, and we need to be gracious to each other inside and outside of the bedroom.

16. Balance Hormones
Consult a reputable naturopath if you suspect hormones are an issue. Avoid synthetic hormone replacements if possible, and use "bioidentical" options instead.

17. Deal with the Things that Turn Off Desire
Whether it's as simple as putting a lock on the bedroom door, or as difficult as reducing stress, find ways to mitigate the turn-offs in your world.

18. More Things that Increase Desire or Make It Easier to be Turned On
A relaxing evening bath, earlier bedtime for the kids, time together just holding hands and talking, an evening walk, whatever helps.

19. Talk with Trusted Friends About Sex and Intimacy
For women, talking with friends about sex, (regular, respectful, open, and non- judgmental conversations), actually increases desire. Get a small group together and all of your marriages benefit.

20. Do Not Tolerate or Attempt to Compete with Porn
Pornography is evil, spawned from hatred, violence, and lies. It is degrading and damaging to women, and even dangerous. Sex in marriage is an expression of love, and mutual pleasure.

If your spouse is doing things that scare you or hurt you, that is not normal, acceptable or right. Get to a safe place and get help. If you don't know anyone who can help you, call RAINN (Rape, Abuse, & Incest National Network) – 1-800-656-4673, or another hotline. You can also text the word, Hello, to the Crisis Text Line – 741741. Don't second guess the urge to reach out for help.

Passion Power Up - Intimacy Key

Physical
Sensual proximity or touching such as holding hands, hugging, kissing, caressing, and sexual activity

Emotional
Sharing of personal feelings, accompanied by understanding, affirmation, validation and demonstration of caring

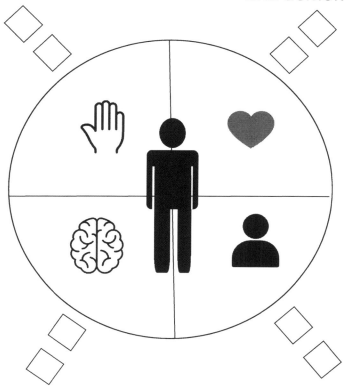

Intellectual
Sharing ideas, thoughts, hopes, dreams, fears, secrets, and experiences

Experiential
Actively engaging in experiences together such as watching a movie, bike riding, going to an amusement park, and dancing

Passion Power Up - Weekly Love Planner

SUNDAY

- [ ]
- [ ]
- [ ]
- [ ]
- [ ]

MONDAY

- [ ]
- [ ]
- [ ]
- [ ]
- [ ]

TUESDAY

- [ ]
- [ ]
- [ ]
- [ ]
- [ ]

WEDNESDAY

- [ ]
- [ ]
- [ ]
- [ ]
- [ ]

THURSDAY

- [ ]
- [ ]
- [ ]
- [ ]
- [ ]

FRIDAY

- [ ]
- [ ]
- [ ]
- [ ]
- [ ]

SATURDAY

- [ ]
- [ ]
- [ ]
- [ ]
- [ ]

INTIMACY KEY

Physical

Emotional

Intellectual

Experiential

Spiritual

Passion Power Up - Intimacy Guide

1. Do your best
2. Communicate your desires
3. Eyes forward and listen
4. Be vulnerable
5. Give your all
6. Ask when you don't know
7. Try new things
8. Reciprocated
9. Work hard and have fun
10. Believe in yourself

Pattern Interrupters

44 De-escalation Strategies & Techniques

- Act calm even if you're not.
- Invite them to do a preferred activity.
- Say, "Let's talk about this later".
- Ask if they can explain more about how they are feeling.
- Use humor to lighten the mood.
- Try to understand the person's perspective.
- Lower your voice.
- Slow yourself down to avoid getting worked up.
- Give a choice.
- Say, "So, you're upset because...right?"
- Walk away but say when you will be back.
- Don't say "calm down".
- Ask, "What would help you right now?"
- Show empathy.
- Change the subject to a positive one.
- Encourage the person to use a coping strategy.
- Show that you are listening.
- Ask if you could hug them.
- Say, "I want to help".
- Remove the audience.
- Give personal space.
- Talk about something they like.
- Clarify expectations.
- Use affirmations.
- Encourage the person to take a walk or journal.
- Give the person an "OUT"(ex. letting them go to another room or a time-out).
- Acknowledge where you agree with the person.
- Coach the person with positive remarks.
- Tell the person, "I am here for you".
- Remind them of something amazing they did.
- Offer to change the way you are doing something.
- Re-state what the person is saying.
- Say, "Talk to me," and really listen.
- Look past the behavior, look for the hurt.
- Be respectful in your tone.
- Spend time de-briefing after the incident to identify ways to improve.
- Avoid needing to get the last word.
- Validate their thoughts and their feelings.
- Avoid over-reacting.
- Offer a solution.
- Apologize for something you did wrong or the way it was taken.
- Say, "I see your point".
- Ask, "Would it help if...?"
- Encourage the person.

44

8 Week Guide for Creating Admiration & Affection

Daily Tools for Cultivating Deeper Connection and Intimacy

Research has found 94 percent of the time that couples who put a positive spin on their marriage's history are likely to have a happy future as well. When happy memories are distorted, it's a sign that the marriage needs help.

In order to have a connected relationship, you must have fondness and regard for one another. Even while you struggle with each other's imperfections, remembering your partner's great characteristics enhances your bond.

It's easier to discuss concerns and execute solutions when you have a stronger bond. Antidotes to contempt include affection and admiration. When you disagree, maintaining a sense of respect for your spouse might help you avoid the "Four Horsemen", key indicators of relational unhappiness and divorce (contempt, criticism, defensiveness, and stonewalling).

The admiration and affection aspects of couple relatedness are the antidote to contempt - it is a buffer to stressors due to a fundamentally positive view of each other.

Sometimes couples resist searching for and expressing gratitude for their spouse's positive behavior doing so feels "phony" to them. But developing a positive habit doesn't "sugarcoat" a relationship. Instead, it resets it to a more realistic perspective. Research suggests just knowing this can make all the difference for couples who are feeling pessimistic about their partner and marriage.

If your feelings for your partner are diminishing, you can do the activities below to help them come back. The route to bringing back positive feelings of affection always begins with realizing how valuable they are. The exercises, as basic as they may appear, have great power. You can repeat them as frequently as you like. Working through the exercises with your partner if your relationship is already happy is a great approach to strengthen it.

Recite the new thought often throughout the day and complete the assignment.

WEEK 1

Monday

New thought: In this partnership, I have a genuine sense of "we" rather than "I."

Assignment: Write about something you and your partner share in common.

_____

_____

Tuesday

New thought: We share many of the same values and views.

Assignment: Describe a shared belief.

_____

_____

Wednesday

New thought: We have similar goals and objectives

Assignment: Make a list of 3 goals.

_____

_____

Thursday

New thought: My partner is the best friend I've ever had.

Assignment: What secret about you does your partner know?

_____

_____

Friday

New thought: In this marriage, I have a lot of support.

Assignment: Write about a time when your partner was extremely helpful to you.

_____

WEEK 2

Monday

New thought: We are able to plan properly and feel in control of our lives as a couple.

Assignment: Describe something you and your partner have planned together.

_____

_____

Tuesday

New thought: I am proud of this relationship.

Assignment: Make a list of two things you're proud of in this relationship.

_____

_____

Wednesday

New thought: I dislike some aspects of my relationship, but I can deal with them.

Assignment: What is one flaw that you have learned to live with?

_____

_____

Thursday

New thought: My family makes me proud.

Assignment: Think of and write about a time when you felt particularly proud.

_____

_____

Friday

New thought: This partnership is a lot better than the majority of those I've witnessed.

Assignment: Consider and write about a bad relationship you know.

_____

_____

WEEK 3

Monday

New thought: Our home is a safe haven where we can get support and relax.

Assignment: List an example when your partner assisted you in reducing stress.

_____

_____

Tuesday

New thought: I vividly recall the first time we met.

Assignment: On paper, describe the first meeting.

_____

_____

Wednesday

New thought: I recall the specifics of our decision to become committed.

Assignment: Write a statement that describes what you remember.

_____

_____

Thursday

New thought: I can remember our wedding and honeymoon.

Assignment: Describe one aspect about them you enjoyed.

_____

_____

Friday

New thought: We have a fair distribution of home responsibilities.

Assignment: Describe one of the ways you do this on a regular basis. If you don't do your fair share, choose a chore that you will complete (such as doing laundry).

_____

WEEK 4

Monday

New thought: I am sincerely grateful for my partner.

Assignment: List one characteristic you find loveable or endearing.

_____

_____

Tuesday

New thought: I can recall the good times in our relationship and they matter.

Assignment: Pick one memorable moment and write a sentence about it.

_____

_____

Wednesday

New thought: I can clearly remember loving, special, romantic times in our relationship.

Assignment: Pick one of these moments and describe it below.

_____

_____

Thursday

New thought: I am physically attracted to my spouse.

Assignment: Write about one physical characteristic that you enjoy.

_____

_____

Friday

New thought: My mate has specific qualities that make me proud and I admire.

Assignment: Write down one quality about which you are proud.

_____

_____

WEEK 5

Monday

New thought: In my relationship, there is a lot of love.

Assignment: Consider and write about a memorable trip you and your partner took together.

_____

_____

Tuesday

New thought: My partner is a fascinating individual.

Assignment: Plan a question to ask your friend on something that both of you are interested in.

_____

_____

Wednesday

New thought: We have a good rapport with one another.

Assignment: Write and mail a love letter to your partner.

_____

_____

Thursday

New thought: In my partnership, there is a lot of mutual respect.

Assignment: Tell your partner about a time when you admired something that your partner did recently.

_____

_____

Friday

New thought: I would marry the same person if I could do it all over again.

Assignment: Plan an anniversary (or other) getaway.

WEEK 6

Monday

New thought: We find one another to be good companions.

Assignment: Plan an excursion or outing together.

_____

_____

Tuesday

New thought: We have a real interest in each other.

Assignment: Write something intriguing to accomplish or talk about that would be interesting.

_____

_____

Wednesday

New thought: We have a lot of affection for one another.

Assignment: Plan a romantic surprise or gift for your partner tonight.

_____

_____

Thursday

New thought: Relationships can be difficult at times. But it's worth it.

Assignment: Write about a difficult moment you and your partner successfully endured together.

_____

_____

Friday

New thought: I was quite blessed when I met my partner.

Assignment: Make a list of one advantage of being in a relationship with your significant other.

_____

WEEK 7

Monday

New thought: We have mutual respect for one another that runs deep.

Assignment: Be mindful of how you speak to each other today. Regard your spouse's ideas, opinions and preferences.

_____

_____

Tuesday

New thought: I feel accepted and liked by my partner.

Assignment: Write something that makes you feel liked by your spouse, let them know.

_____

_____

Wednesday

New thought: My partner really enjoys my achievements and accomplishments.

Assignment: What is one thing you have accomplished together? Write and reflect.

_____

_____

Thursday

New thought: We validate each other well, because we matter to each other.

Assignment: Intentionally validate your spouse today.

_____

_____

Friday

New thought: We rarely go to sleep without some show of love and affection.

Assignment: Make a list of three ways you show your spouse love and affection. Share.

_____

WEEK 8

Monday

New thought: My mate can be very adorable.

Assignment: Get dressed up for an elegant evening together. Or, plan another kind of evening out you would enjoy.

_____

_____

Tuesday

New thought: We find each other's sense of humor amusing.

Assignment: The assignment is to watch a comedy film together. Make a note of the title here.

_____

_____

Wednesday

New thought: In this relationship, sex is generally (or can be) quite satisfying.

Assignment: Plan an erotic evening for you and your partner.

_____

_____

Thursday

New thought: We have come a long way together.

Assignment: Make a list of all you've accomplished as a team.

_____

_____

Friday

New thought: I believe we will be able to weather any storm together.

Assignment: Reminisce about how you overcame adversity. Share.

_____

ISBN: 978-0-9983999-5-9 (Paperback)

Any references to historical events, real people, or real places are used fictitiously. Names, characters, and places are products of the author's imagination.

Unless otherwise indicated, Scripture quotations are taken from the New American Standard Bible (NASB), © 1960, 1977, 1995 by the Lockman Foundation.

Other Scripture quotations are taken from the following sources:

The New King James Version of the Bible (KJV). The New King James Bible (NKJV ®), copyright © 1982 by Thomas Nelson, Inc. The Holy Bible, English Standard Version TM (ESV) copyright 2001 by Crossway Bibles, a division of Good News Publishers. All rights reserved. New International Reader's Version (NIRV) copyright © 1996, 1998 by International Bible Society. All rights reserved worldwide. The Holy Bible, New International Version (NIV). Copyright © 1973, 1978, 1984, International Bible Society. Used by permission.

Front cover image by public domain www.pexels.com. Book design by Relentless Publications, Inc.

Printed by Relentless Publications, Inc., in the United States of America.

First printing edition 2017.

www.MyMarriageIntensive.com www.RelentlessMarriage.com

30059431R00030